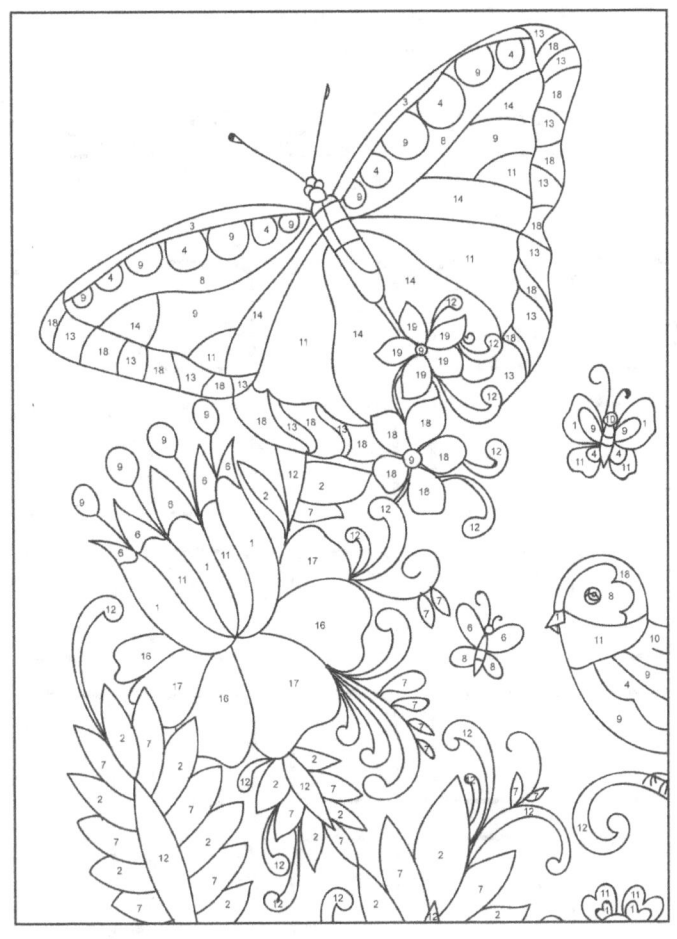

LARGE PRINT
COLOR by NUMBER Butterflies, Birds, and Flowers Adult Coloring Book

By Lilt Kids Coloring Books

COLOR TEST PAGE

COLOR TEST PAGE

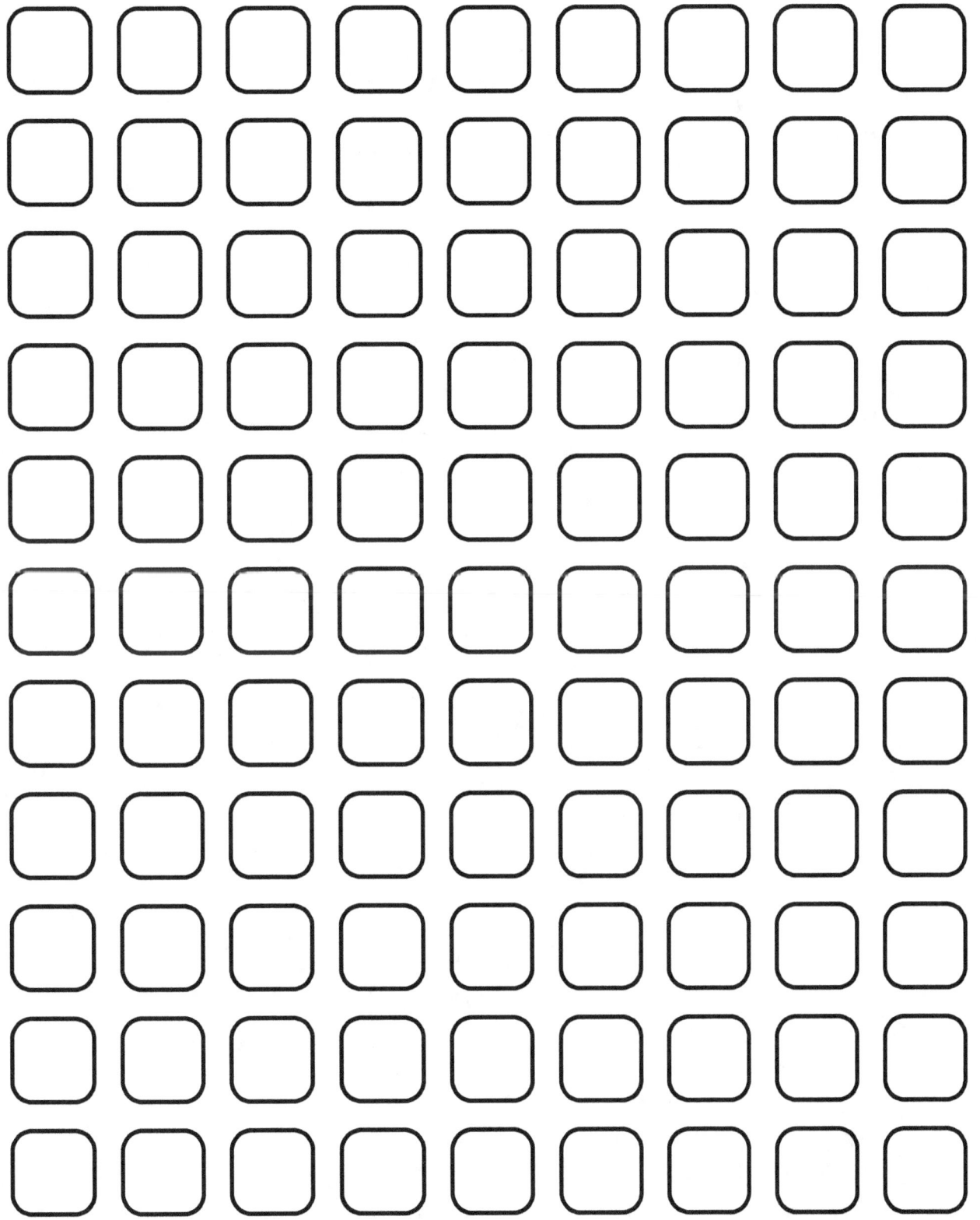

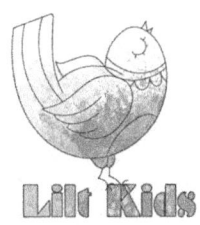

Coloring Tips

1) Relax and Enjoy

Coloring is good for stress relief, anxiety, depression and so much more. There's no wrong way to color. Do it while you watch tv, drink tea, listen to music, or do nothing but focus on the coloring. Don't compare your art to anyone else's. You probably won't love every single page you create, and that's to be expected! If you are enjoying the journey, that's all that matters.

2) Choose the right tools

Colored pencils, crayons, or markers? What you choose to color with is a very personal choice and may evolve over time. If you want to know our favorite brands, visit LiltKids.com/picks for our picks. If you choose markers, we recommend you put a blank sheet of paper behind the page so the colors don't run onto the next image.

3) Color Schemes

Try out your colors in the test pages at the front of this book, and pick out some that might go well together. Need inspiration? Google "color palette generator", you'll find multiple online tools to help you choose colors that go well together.

4) Framing Your Pages

Unfortunately, as a very small publisher we don't yet have the ability to offer perforated pages. However, you can find an inexpensive tool called a page perforator on amazon and turn any coloring book page into a perforated page. Visit Liltkids.com/picks for our recommendation.

5) Share Your Work

We want to see what you create! So do our illustrators. Snap a photo and email us your work: liltkidscoloring@gmail.com.

That's it! Go forth and color.

Art washes away from the soul the dust of everyday life.
— *Pablo Picasso*

1	Red
2	Green
3	Blue
4	Yellow
5	Gold
6	Pink
7	Light Green
8	Light Blue
9	Deep Yellow
10	Brown
11	Dark Red
12	Dark Green
13	Dark Blue
14	Orange
15	Purple
16	Light Violet
17	Violet
18	Cyan
19	Magenta
20	Dark Purple

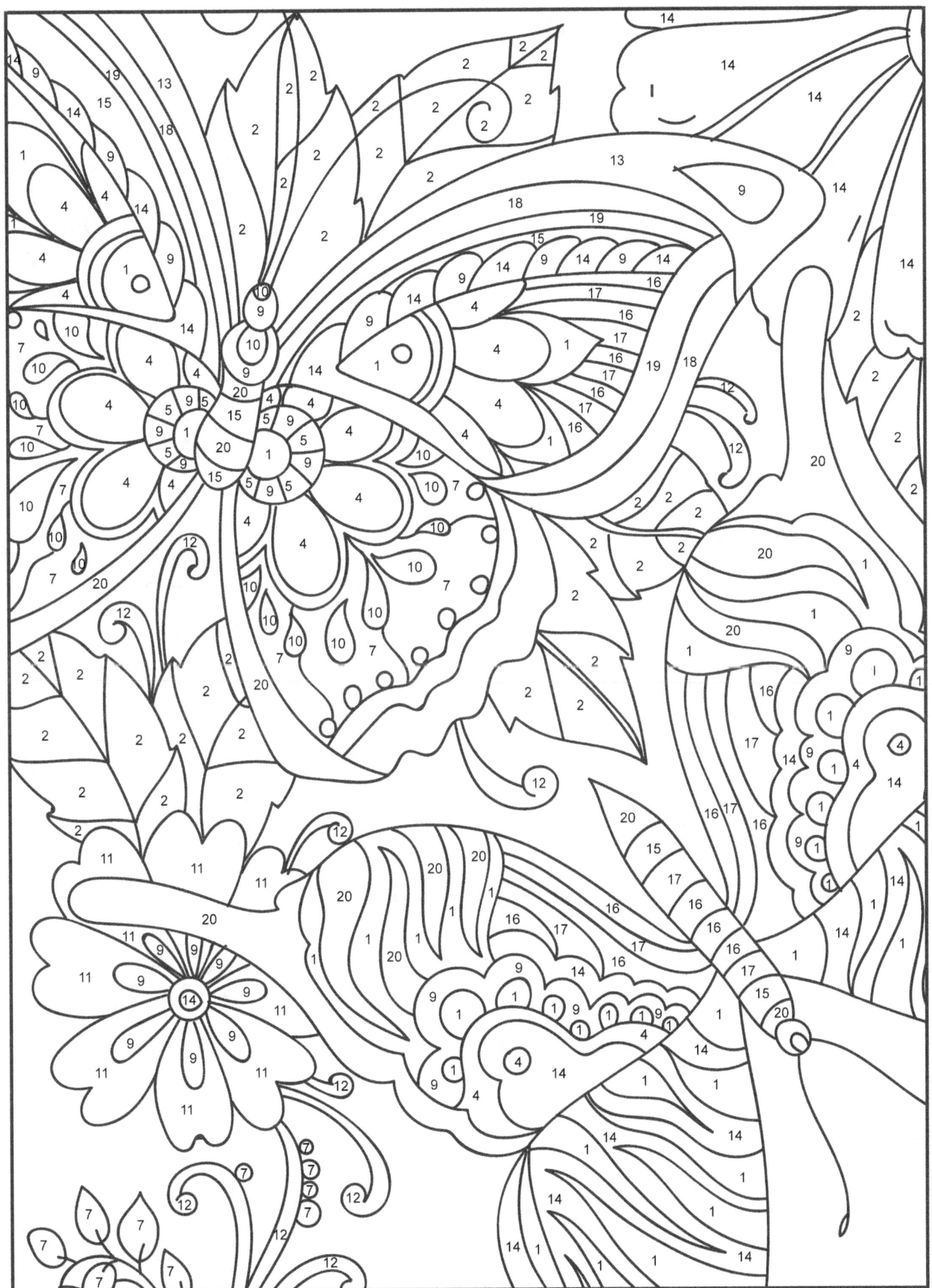

1	Red
2	Green
3	Blue
4	Yellow
5	Gold
6	Pink
7	Light Green
8	Light Blue
9	Deep Yellow
10	Brown
11	Dark Red
12	Dark Green
13	Dark Blue
14	Orange
15	Purple
16	Light Violet
17	Violet
18	Cyan
19	Magenta
20	Dark Purple

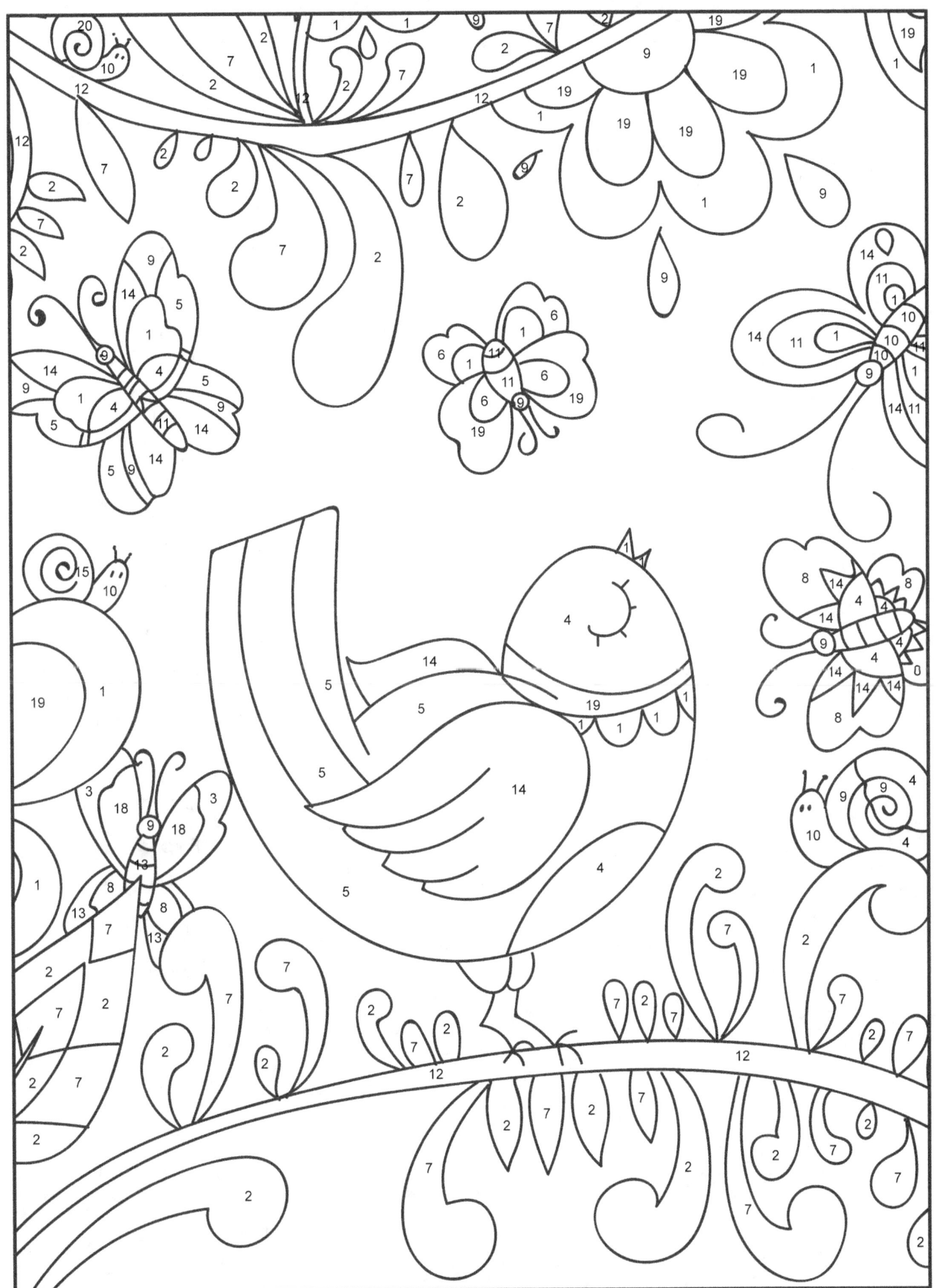

1	Red
2	Green
3	Blue
4	Yellow
5	Gold
6	Pink
7	Light Green
8	Light Blue
9	Deep Yellow
10	Brown
11	Dark Red
12	Dark Green
13	Dark Blue
14	Orange
15	Purple
16	Light Violet
17	Violet
18	Cyan
19	Magenta
20	Dark Purple

1	Red
2	Green
3	Blue
4	Yellow
5	Gold
6	Pink
7	Light Green
8	Light Blue
9	Deep Yellow
10	Brown
11	Dark Red
12	Dark Green
13	Dark Blue
14	Orange
15	Purple
16	Light Violet
17	Violet
18	Cyan
19	Magenta
20	Dark Purple

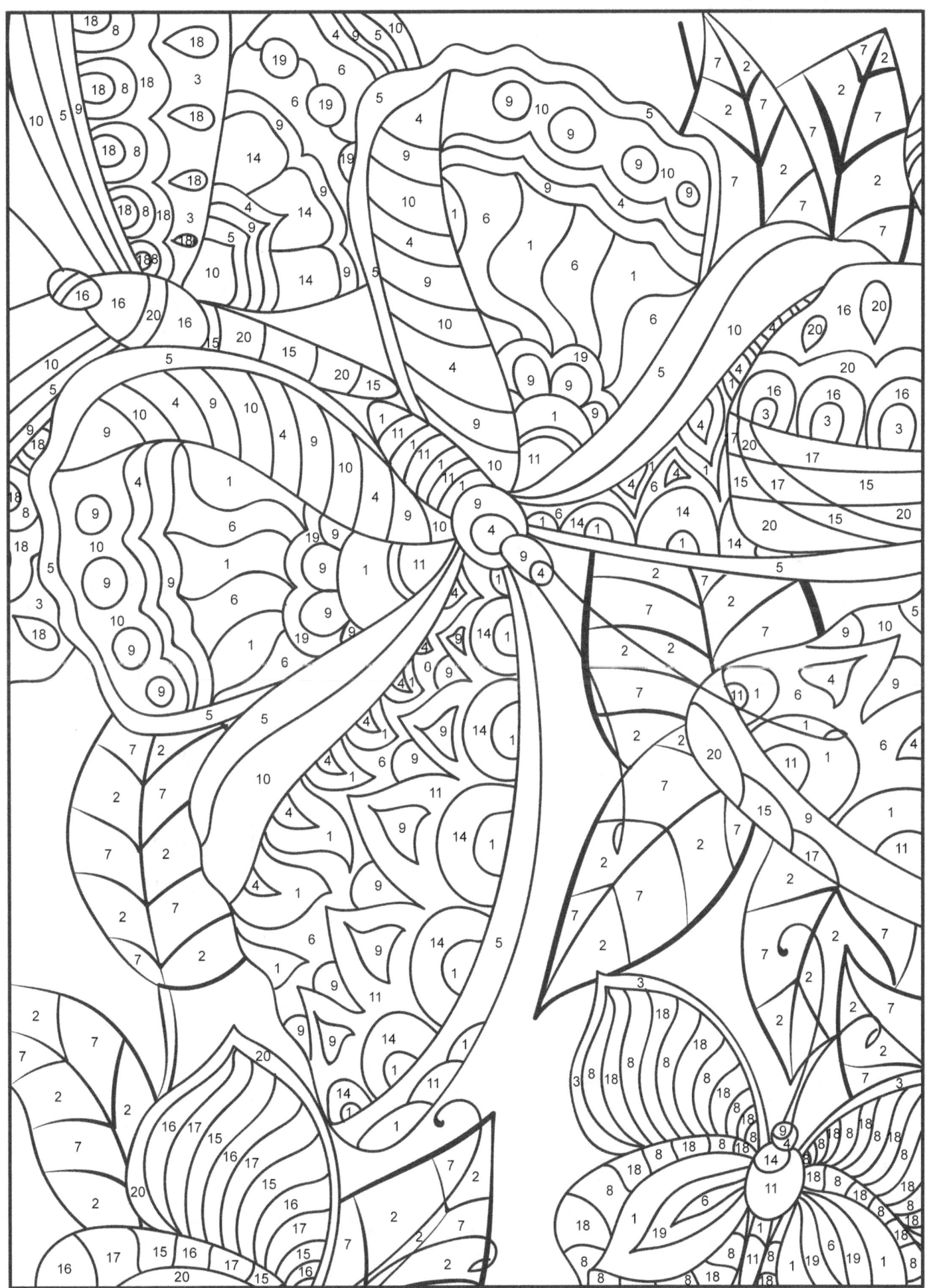

1	Red
2	Green
3	Blue
4	Yellow
5	Gold
6	Pink
7	Light Green
8	Light Blue
9	Deep Yellow
10	Brown
11	Dark Red
12	Dark Green
13	Dark Blue
14	Orange
15	Purple
16	Light Violet
17	Violet
18	Cyan
19	Magenta
20	Dark Purple

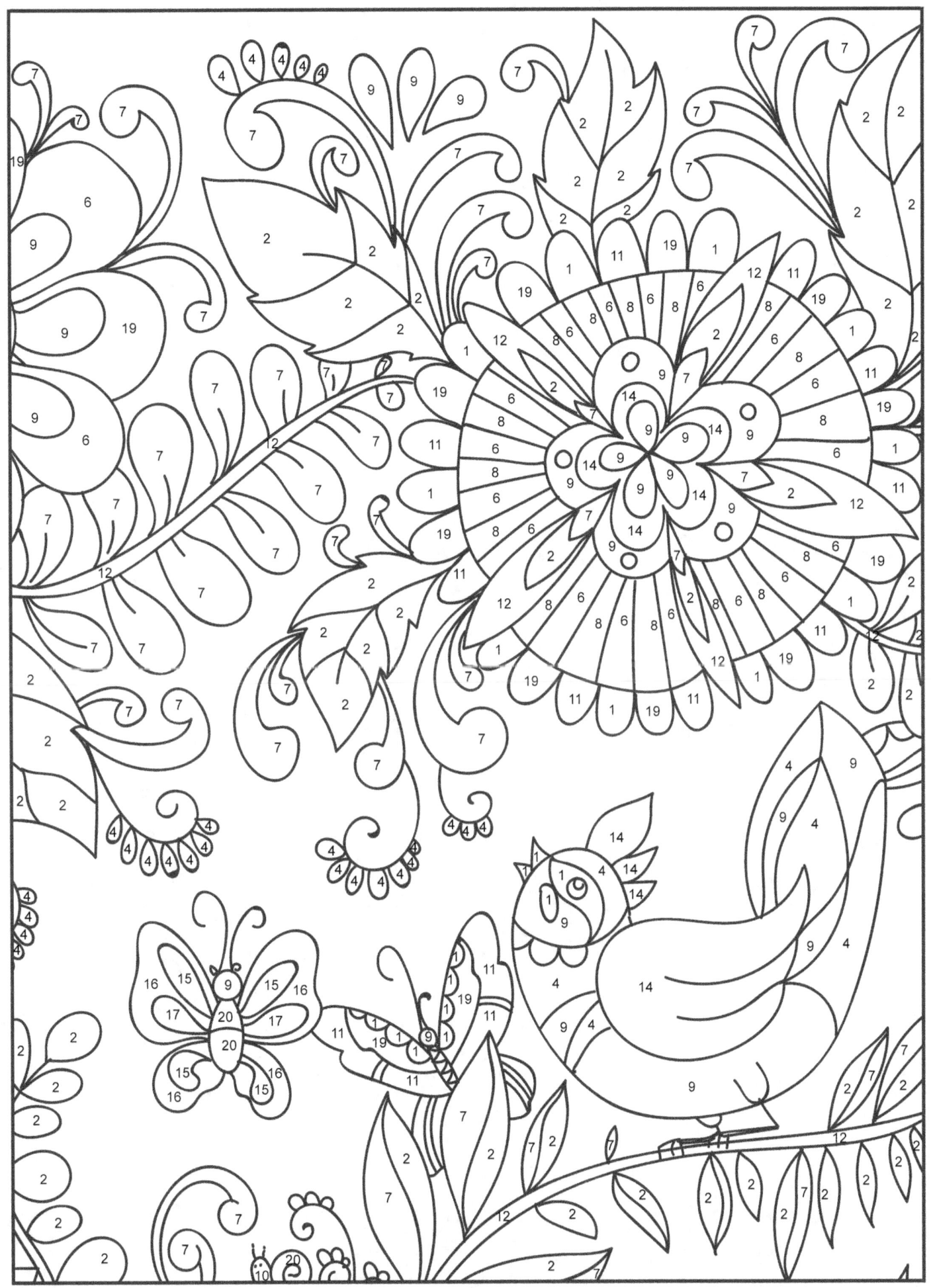

1	Red
2	Green
3	Blue
4	Yellow
5	Gold
6	Pink
7	Light Green
8	Light Blue
9	Deep Yellow
10	Brown
11	Dark Red
12	Dark Green
13	Dark Blue
14	Orange
15	Purple
16	Light Violet
17	Violet
18	Cyan
19	Magenta
20	Dark Purple

1	Red
2	Green
3	Blue
4	Yellow
5	Gold
6	Pink
7	Light Green
8	Light Blue
9	Deep Yellow
10	Brown
11	Dark Red
12	Dark Green
13	Dark Blue
14	Orange
15	Purple
16	Light Violet
17	Violet
18	Cyan
19	Magenta
20	Dark Purple

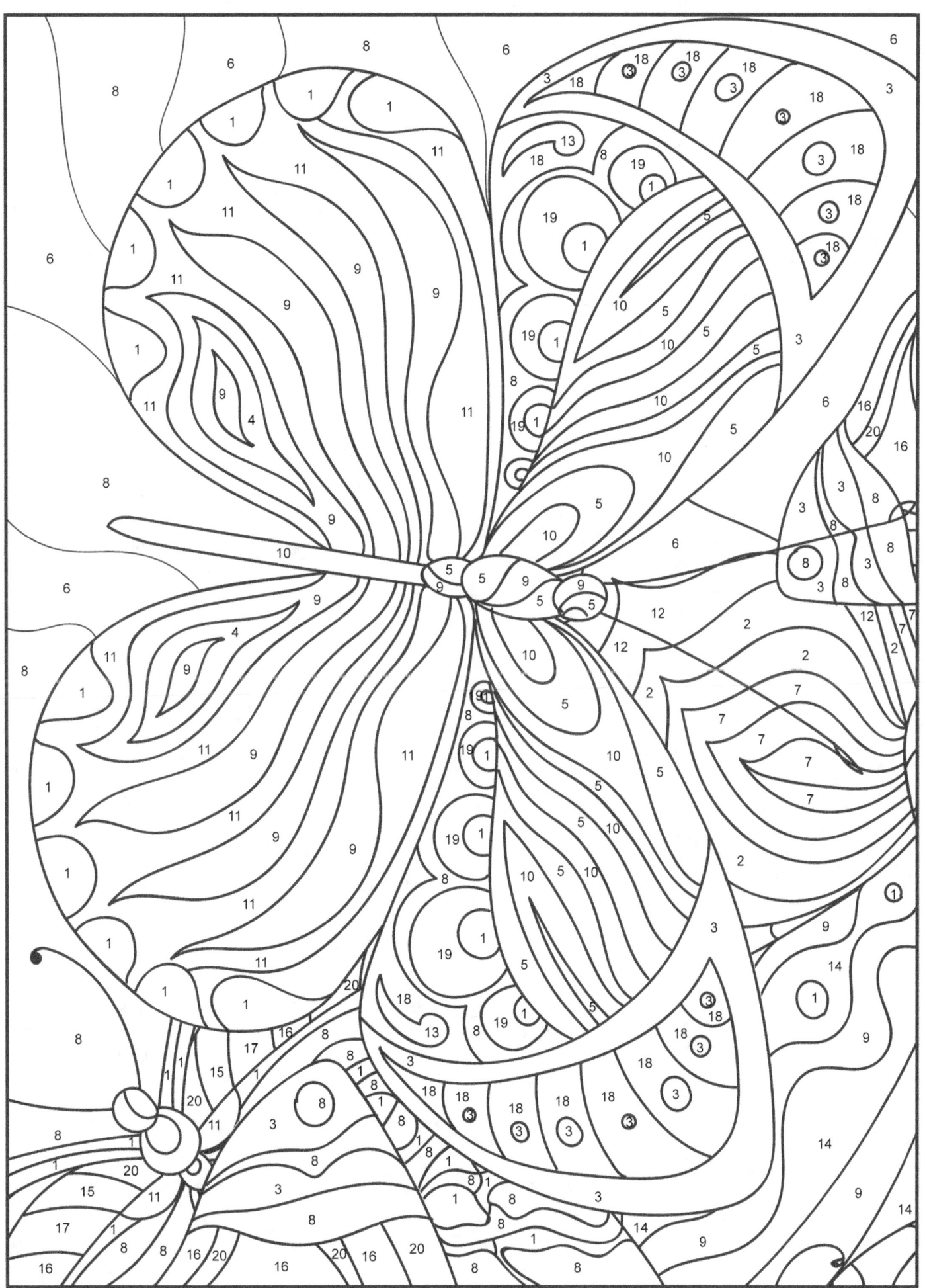

1	Red
2	Green
3	Blue
4	Yellow
5	Gold
6	Pink
7	Light Green
8	Light Blue
9	Deep Yellow
10	Brown
11	Dark Red
12	Dark Green
13	Dark Blue
14	Orange
15	Purple
16	Light Violet
17	Violet
18	Cyan
19	Magenta
20	Dark Purple

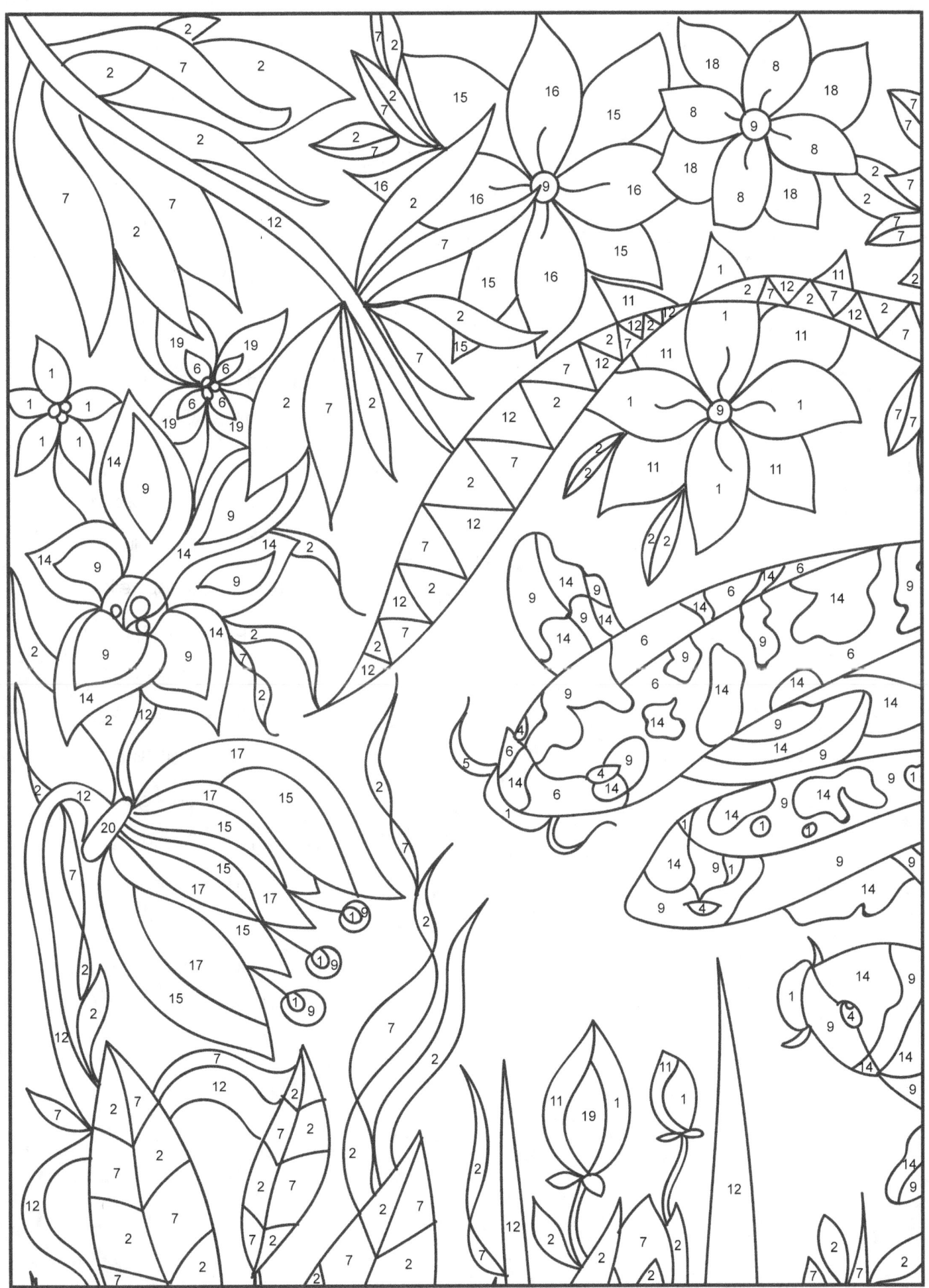

1	Red
2	Green
3	Blue
4	Yellow
5	Gold
6	Pink
7	Light Green
8	Light Blue
9	Deep Yellow
10	Brown
11	Dark Red
12	Dark Green
13	Dark Blue
14	Orange
15	Purple
16	Light Violet
17	Violet
18	Cyan
19	Magenta
20	Dark Purple

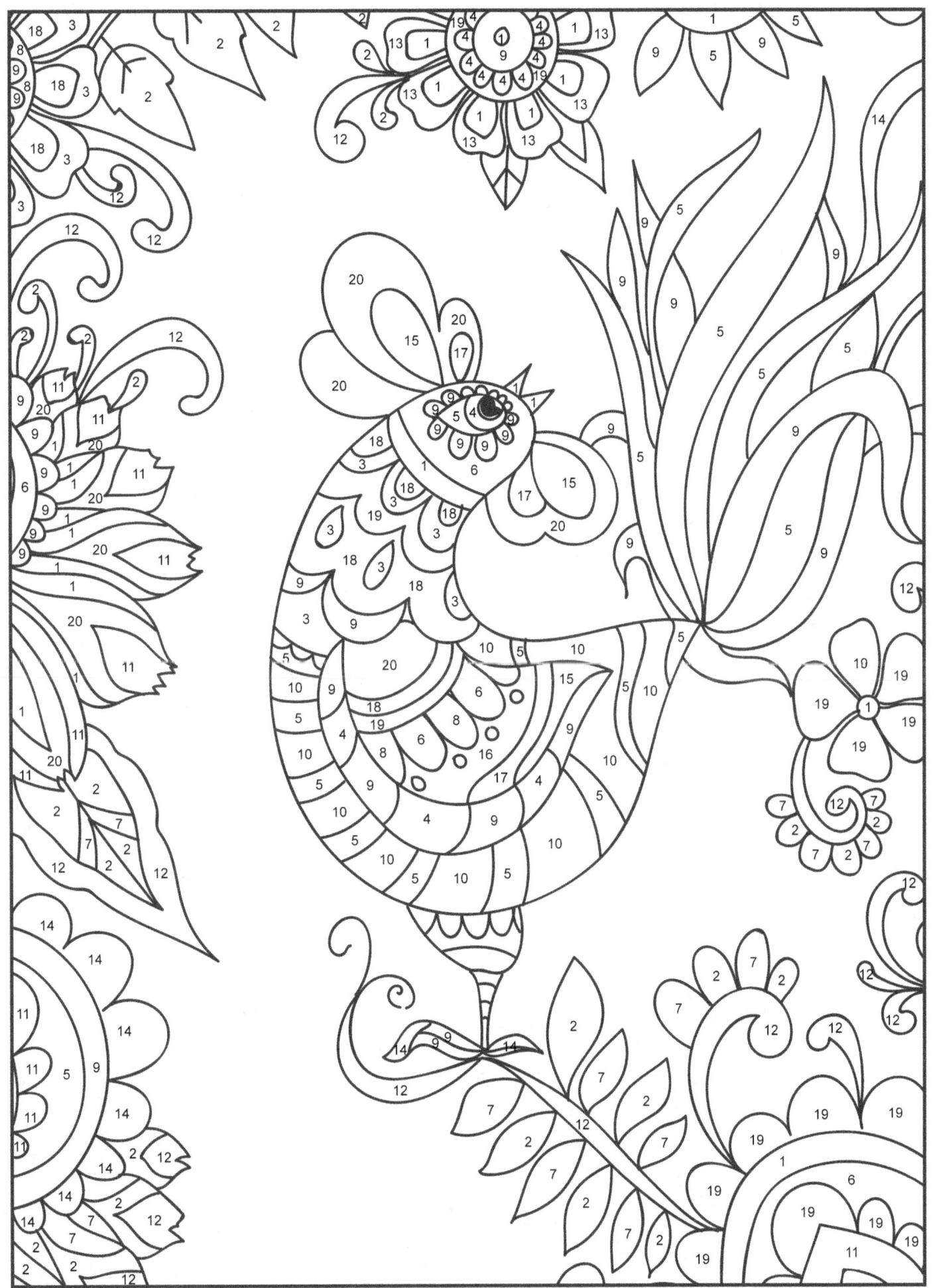

1	Red
2	Green
3	Blue
4	Yellow
5	Gold
6	Pink
7	Light Green
8	Light Blue
9	Deep Yellow
10	Brown
11	Dark Red
12	Dark Green
13	Dark Blue
14	Orange
15	Purple
16	Light Violet
17	Violet
18	Cyan
19	Magenta
20	Dark Purple

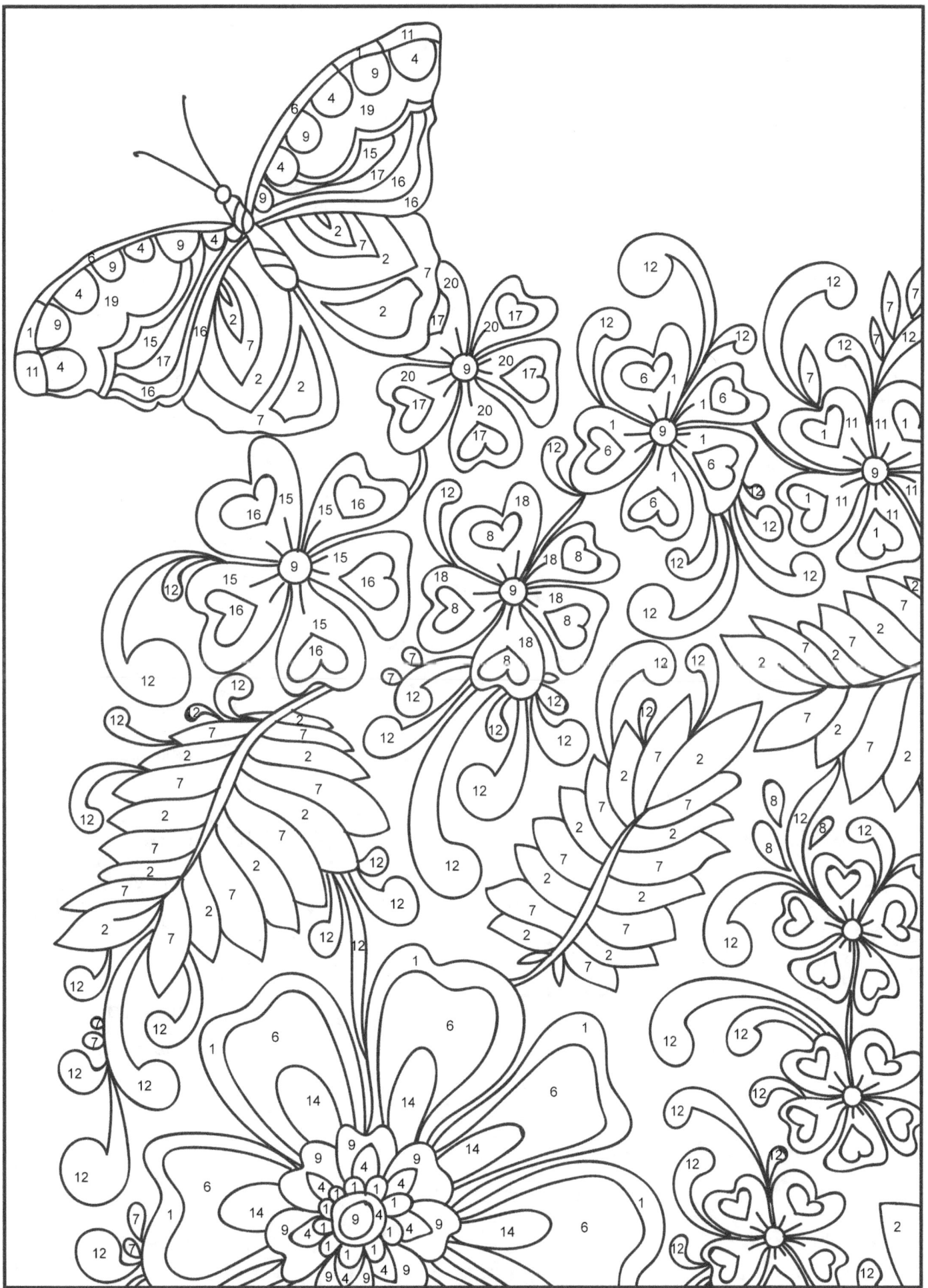

1	Red
2	Green
3	Blue
4	Yellow
5	Gold
6	Pink
7	Light Green
8	Light Blue
9	Deep Yellow
10	Brown
11	Dark Red
12	Dark Green
13	Dark Blue
14	Orange
15	Purple
16	Light Violet
17	Violet
18	Cyan
19	Magenta
20	Dark Purple

1	Red
2	Green
3	Blue
4	Yellow
5	Gold
6	Pink
7	Light Green
8	Light Blue
9	Deep Yellow
10	Brown
11	Dark Red
12	Dark Green
13	Dark Blue
14	Orange
15	Purple
16	Light Violet
17	Violet
18	Cyan
19	Magenta
20	Dark Purple

1	Red
2	Green
3	Blue
4	Yellow
5	Gold
6	Pink
7	Light Green
8	Light Blue
9	Deep Yellow
10	Brown
11	Dark Red
12	Dark Green
13	Dark Blue
14	Orange
15	Purple
16	Light Violet
17	Violet
18	Cyan
19	Magenta
20	Dark Purple

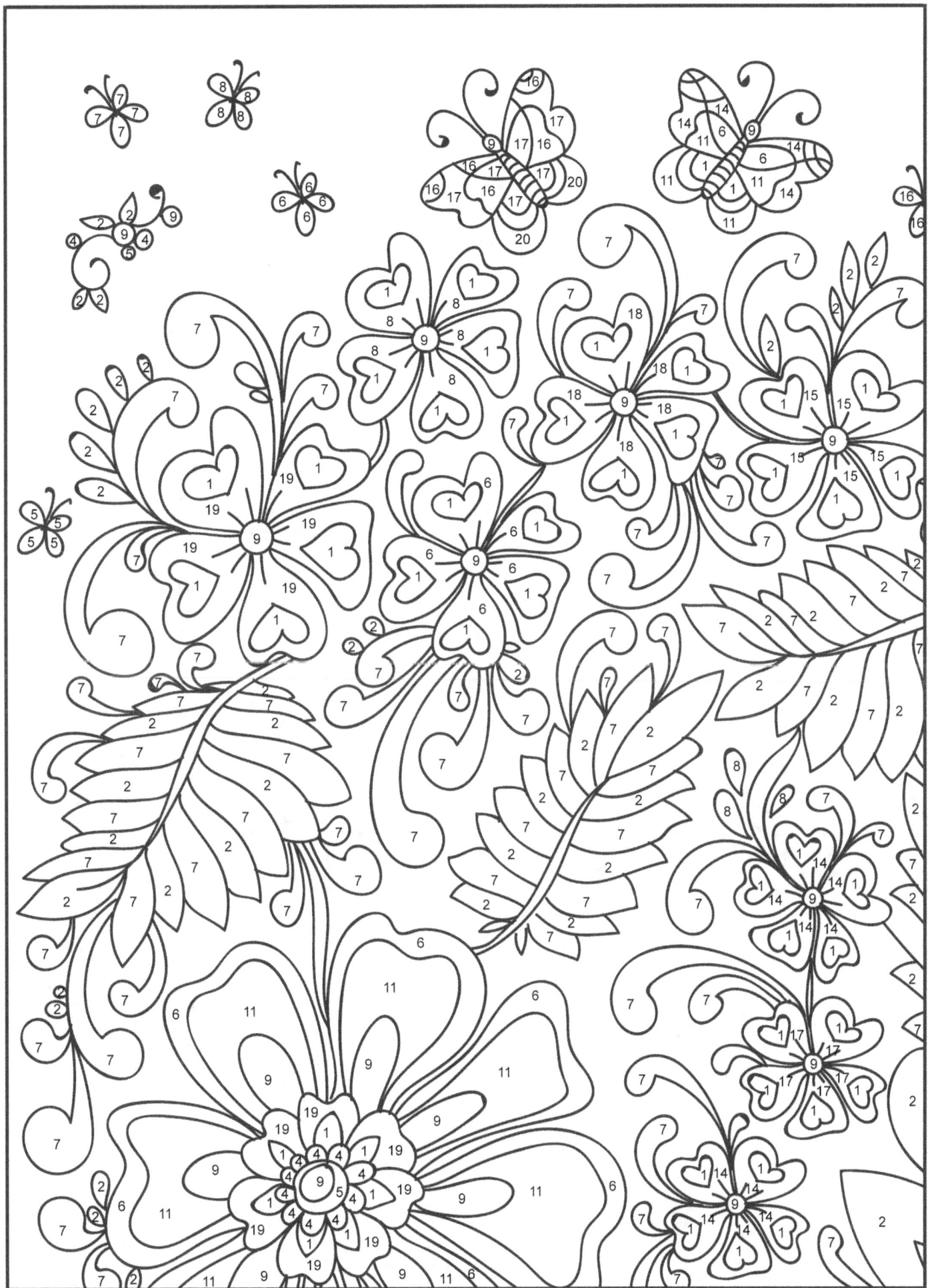

1	Red
2	Green
3	Blue
4	Yellow
5	Gold
6	Pink
7	Light Green
8	Light Blue
9	Deep Yellow
10	Brown
11	Dark Red
12	Dark Green
13	Dark Blue
14	Orange
15	Purple
16	Light Violet
17	Violet
18	Cyan
19	Magenta
20	Dark Purple

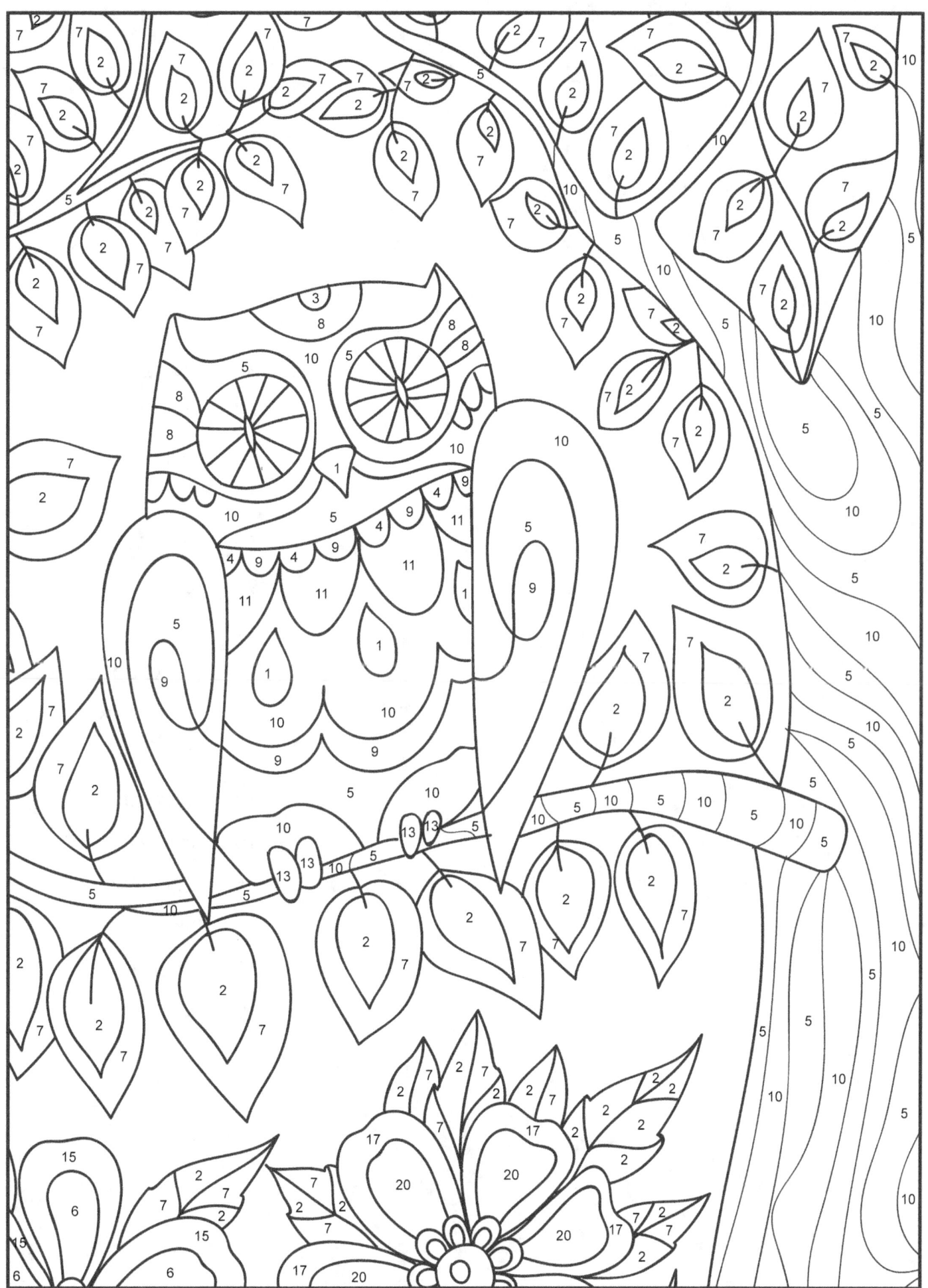

1	Red
2	Green
3	Blue
4	Yellow
5	Gold
6	Pink
7	Light Green
8	Light Blue
9	Deep Yellow
10	Brown
11	Dark Red
12	Dark Green
13	Dark Blue
14	Orange
15	Purple
16	Light Violet
17	Violet
18	Cyan
19	Magenta
20	Dark Purple

1	Red
2	Green
3	Blue
4	Yellow
5	Gold
6	Pink
7	Light Green
8	Light Blue
9	Deep Yellow
10	Brown
11	Dark Red
12	Dark Green
13	Dark Blue
14	Orange
15	Purple
16	Light Violet
17	Violet
18	Cyan
19	Magenta
20	Dark Purple

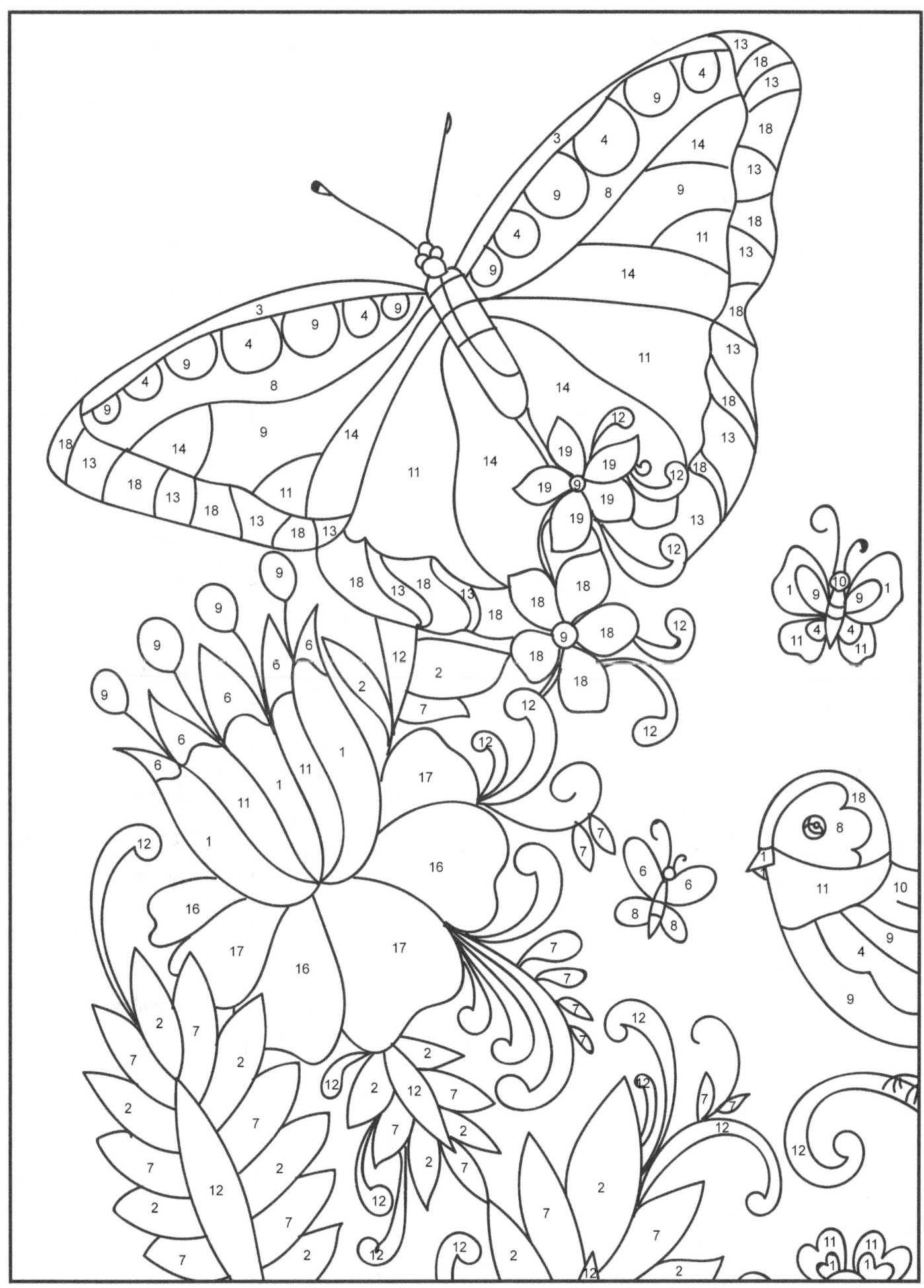

1	Red
2	Green
3	Blue
4	Yellow
5	Gold
6	Pink
7	Light Green
8	Light Blue
9	Deep Yellow
10	Brown
11	Dark Red
12	Dark Green
13	Dark Blue
14	Orange
15	Purple
16	Light Violet
17	Violet
18	Cyan
19	Magenta
20	Dark Purple

1	Red
2	Green
3	Blue
4	Yellow
5	Gold
6	Pink
7	Light Green
8	Light Blue
9	Deep Yellow
10	Brown
11	Dark Red
12	Dark Green
13	Dark Blue
14	Orange
15	Purple
16	Light Violet
17	Violet
18	Cyan
19	Magenta
20	Dark Purple

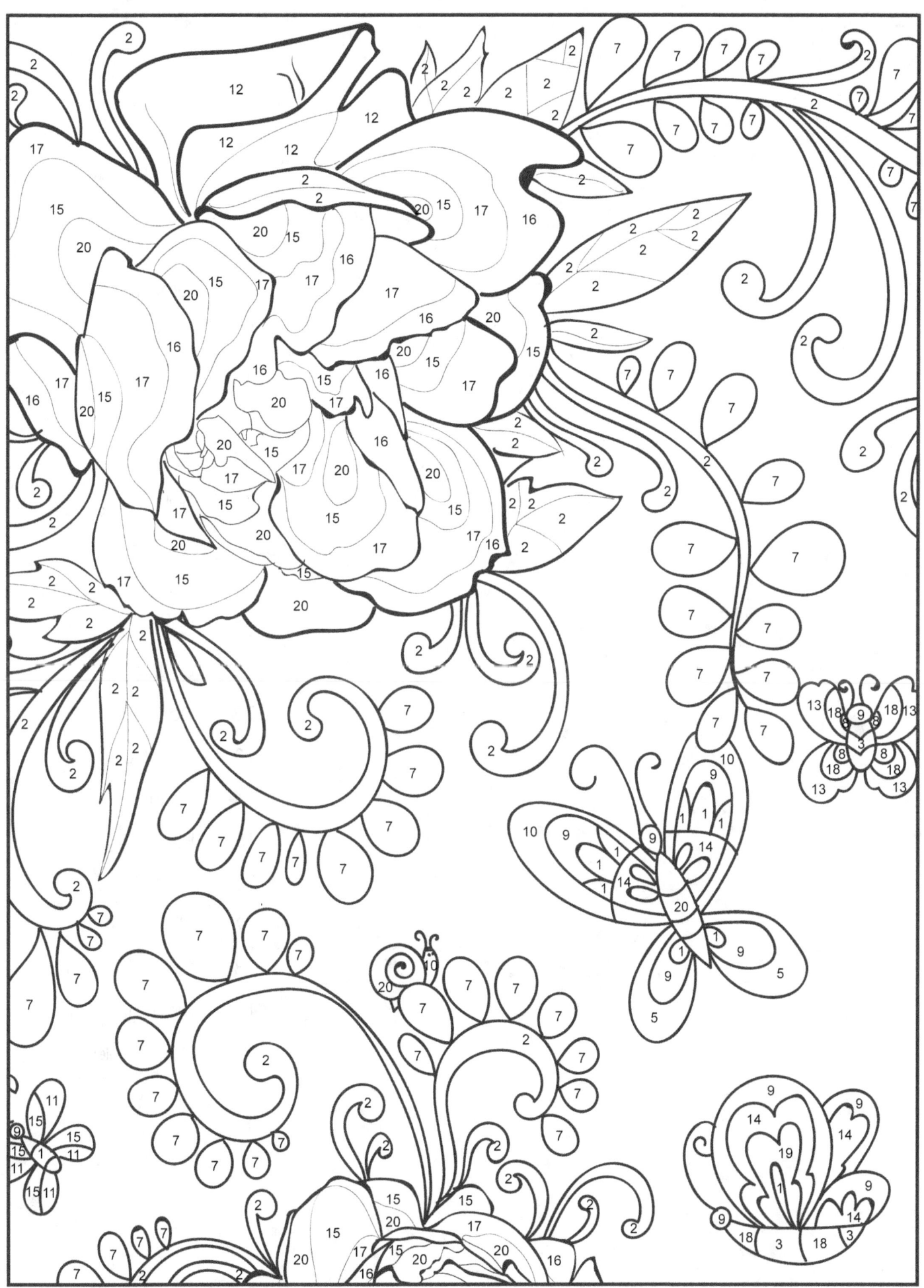

1	Red
2	Green
3	Blue
4	Yellow
5	Gold
6	Pink
7	Light Green
8	Light Blue
9	Deep Yellow
10	Brown
11	Dark Red
12	Dark Green
13	Dark Blue
14	Orange
15	Purple
16	Light Violet
17	Violet
18	Cyan
19	Magenta
20	Dark Purple

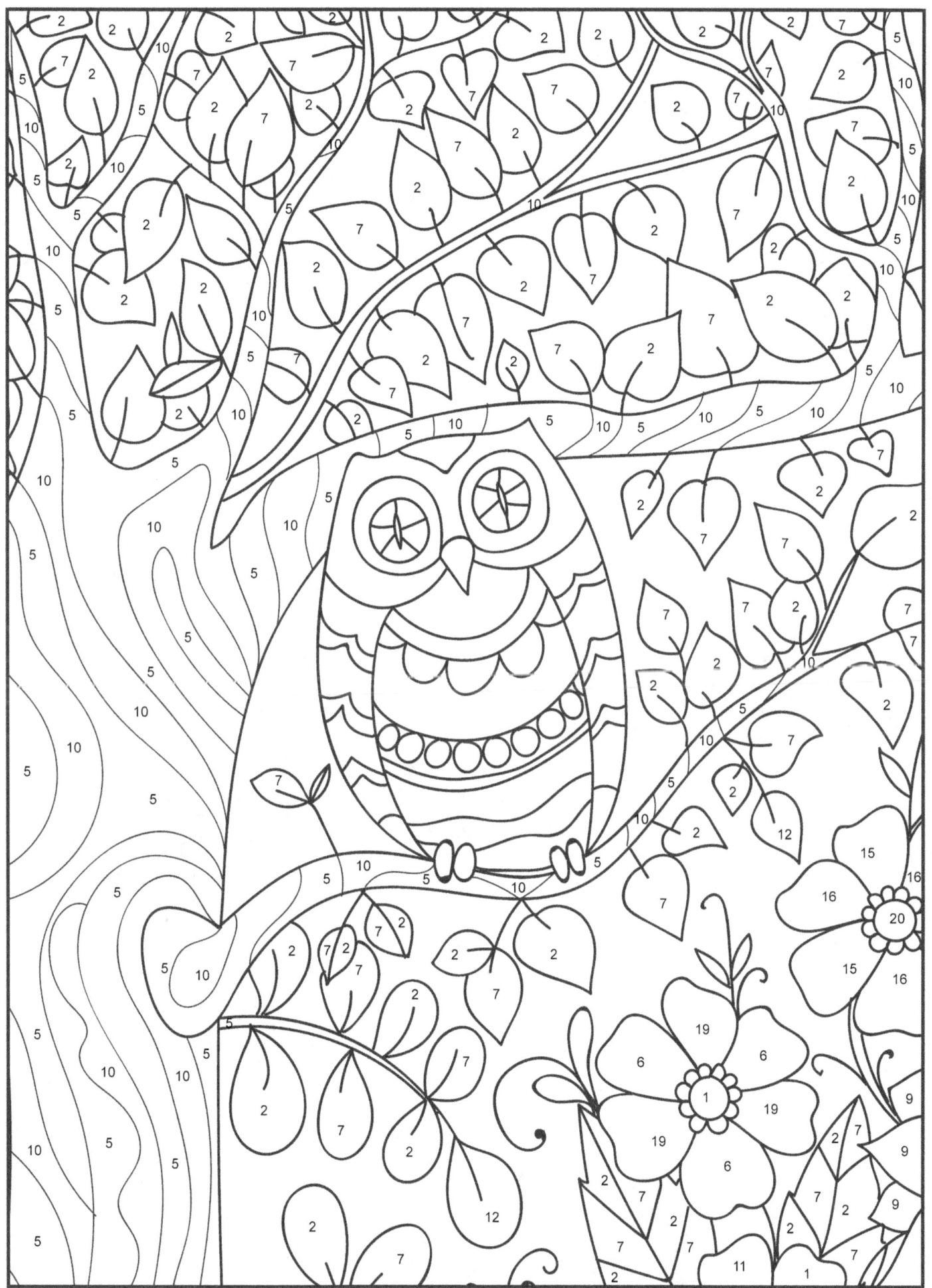

1	Red
2	Green
3	Blue
4	Yellow
5	Gold
6	Pink
7	Light Green
8	Light Blue
9	Deep Yellow
10	Brown
11	Dark Red
12	Dark Green
13	Dark Blue
14	Orange
15	Purple
16	Light Violet
17	Violet
18	Cyan
19	Magenta
20	Dark Purple

1	Red
2	Green
3	Blue
4	Yellow
5	Gold
6	Pink
7	Light Green
8	Light Blue
9	Deep Yellow
10	Brown
11	Dark Red
12	Dark Green
13	Dark Blue
14	Orange
15	Purple
16	Light Violet
17	Violet
18	Cyan
19	Magenta
20	Dark Purple

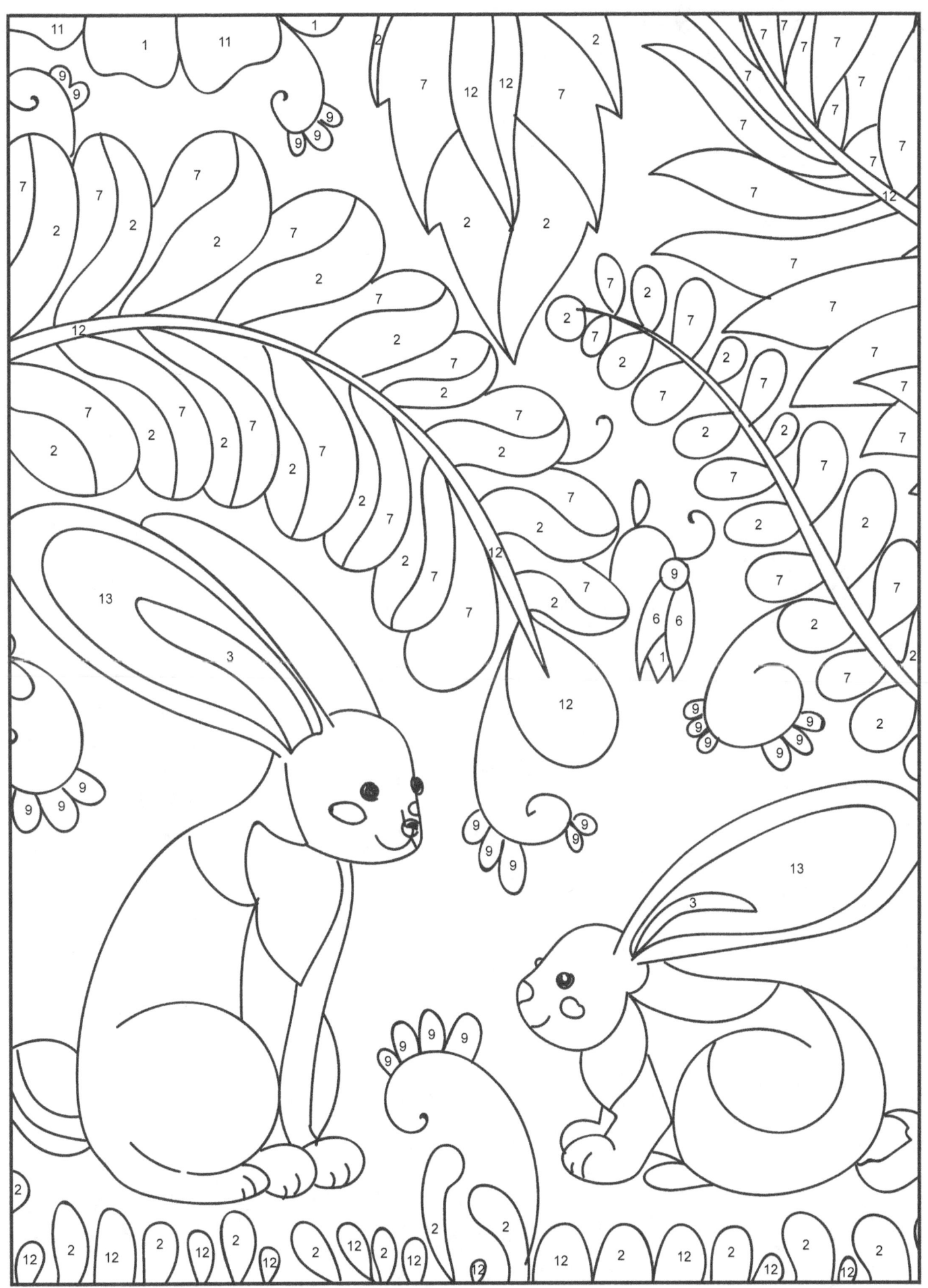

1	Red
2	Green
3	Blue
4	Yellow
5	Gold
6	Pink
7	Light Green
8	Light Blue
9	Deep Yellow
10	Brown
11	Dark Red
12	Dark Green
13	Dark Blue
14	Orange
15	Purple
16	Light Violet
17	Violet
18	Cyan
19	Magenta
20	Dark Purple

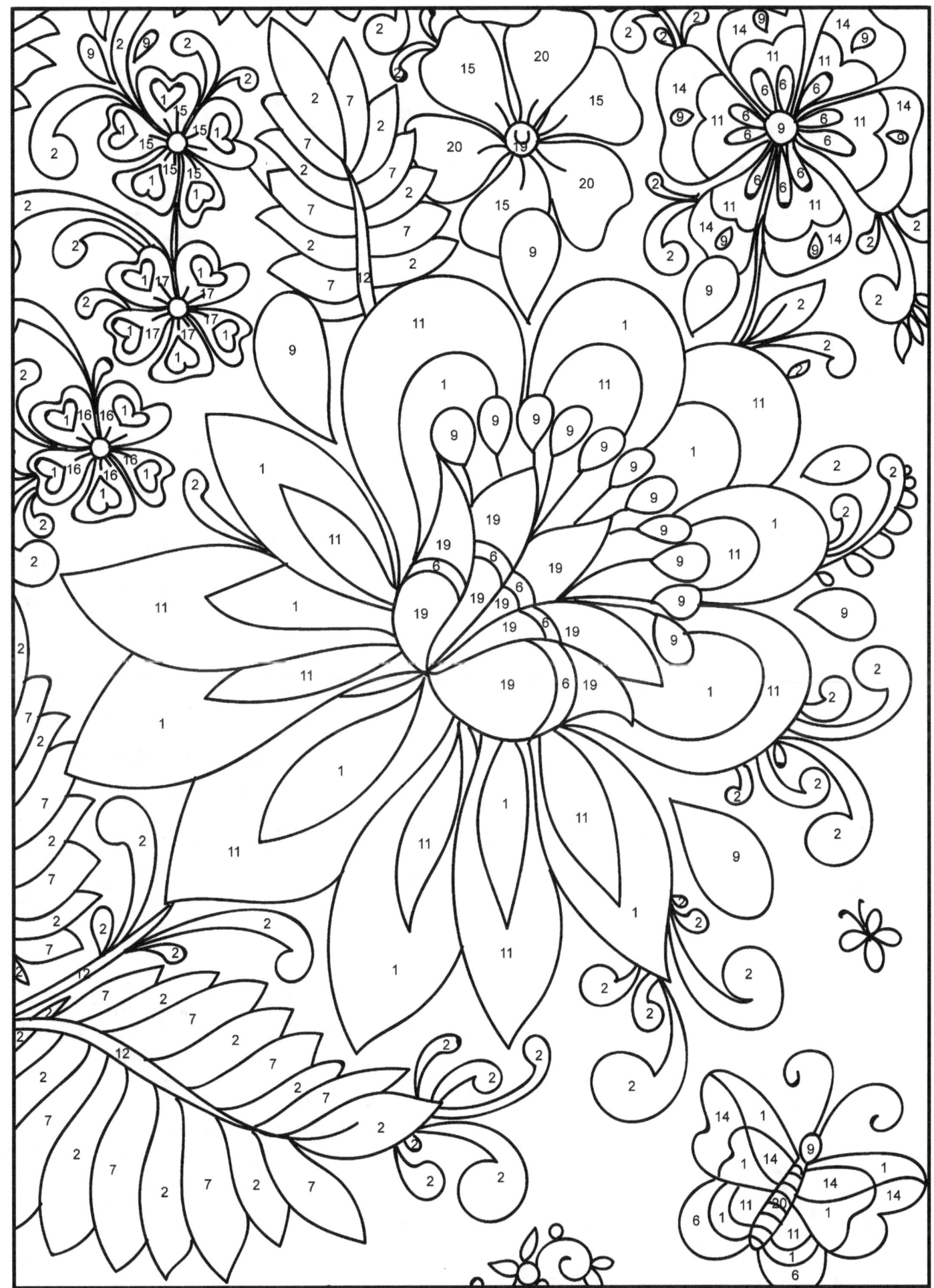

1	Red
2	Green
3	Blue
4	Yellow
5	Gold
6	Pink
7	Light Green
8	Light Blue
9	Deep Yellow
10	Brown
11	Dark Red
12	Dark Green
13	Dark Blue
14	Orange
15	Purple
16	Light Violet
17	Violet
18	Cyan
19	Magenta
20	Dark Purple

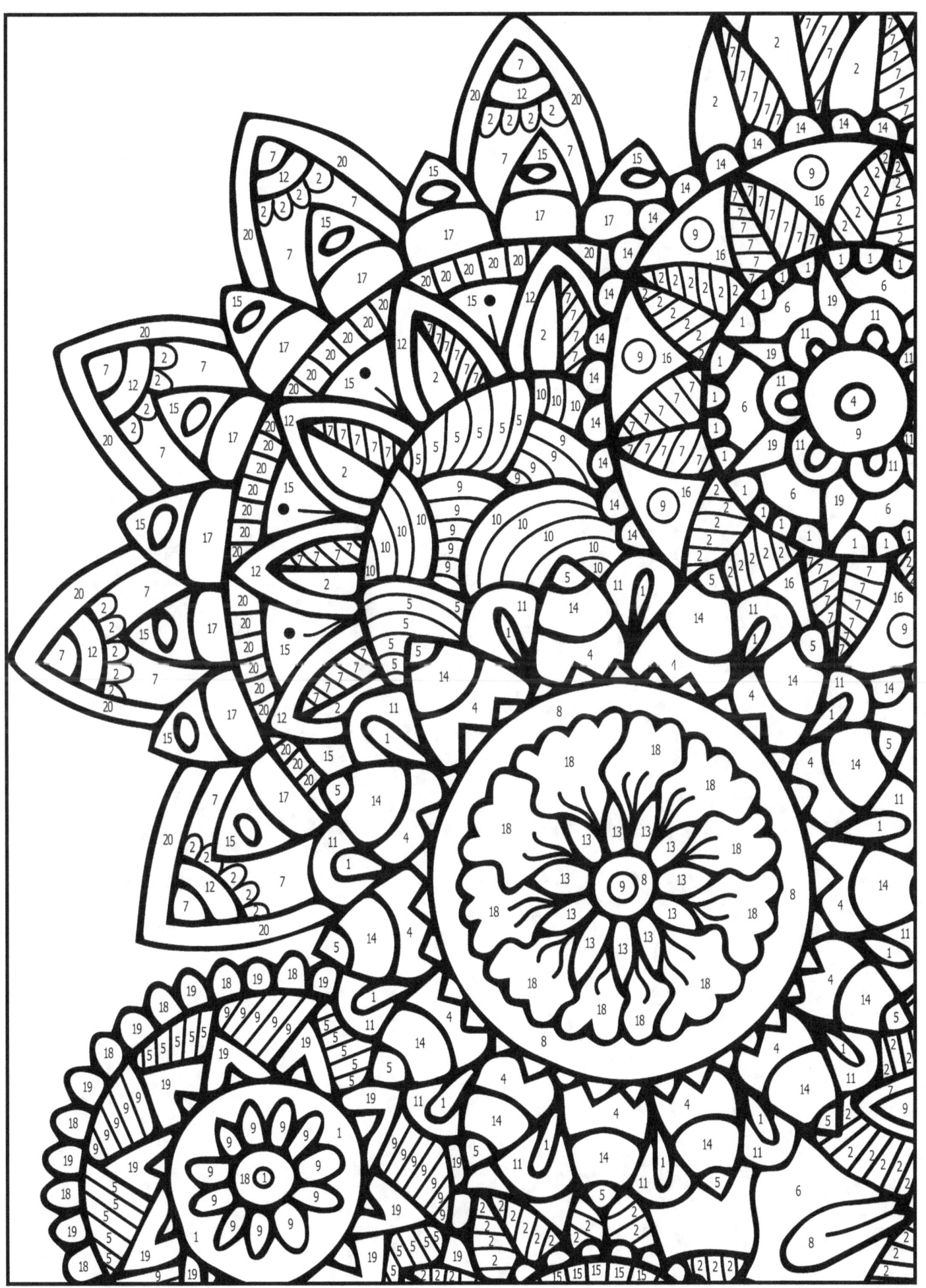

1	Red
2	Green
3	Blue
4	Yellow
5	Gold
6	Pink
7	Light Green
8	Light Blue
9	Deep Yellow
10	Brown
11	Dark Red
12	Dark Green
13	Dark Blue
14	Orange
15	Purple
16	Light Violet
17	Violet
18	Cyan
19	Magenta
20	Dark Purple

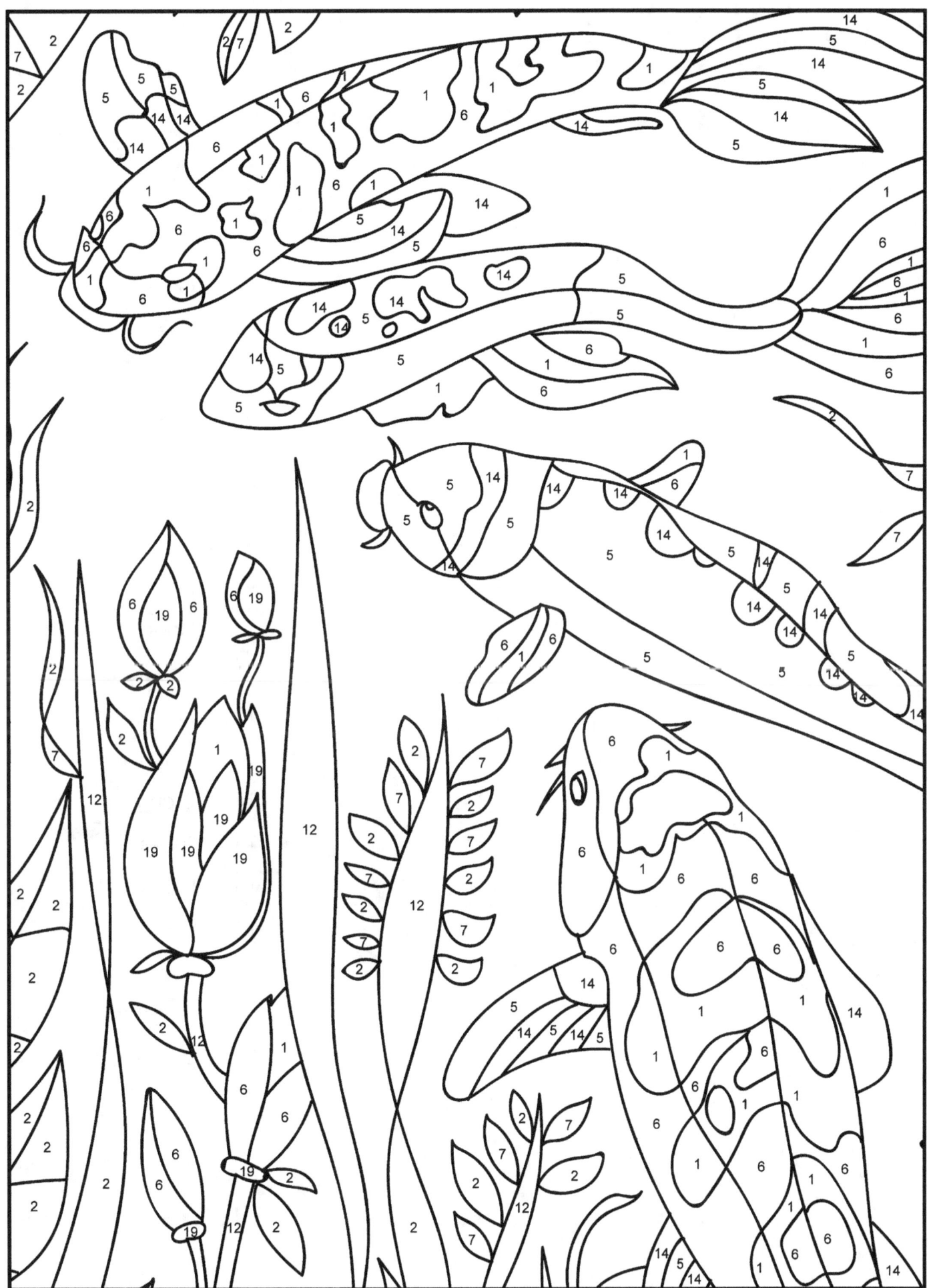

1	Red
2	Green
3	Blue
4	Yellow
5	Gold
6	Pink
7	Light Green
8	Light Blue
9	Deep Yellow
10	Brown
11	Dark Red
12	Dark Green
13	Dark Blue
14	Orange
15	Purple
16	Light Violet
17	Violet
18	Cyan
19	Magenta
20	Dark Purple

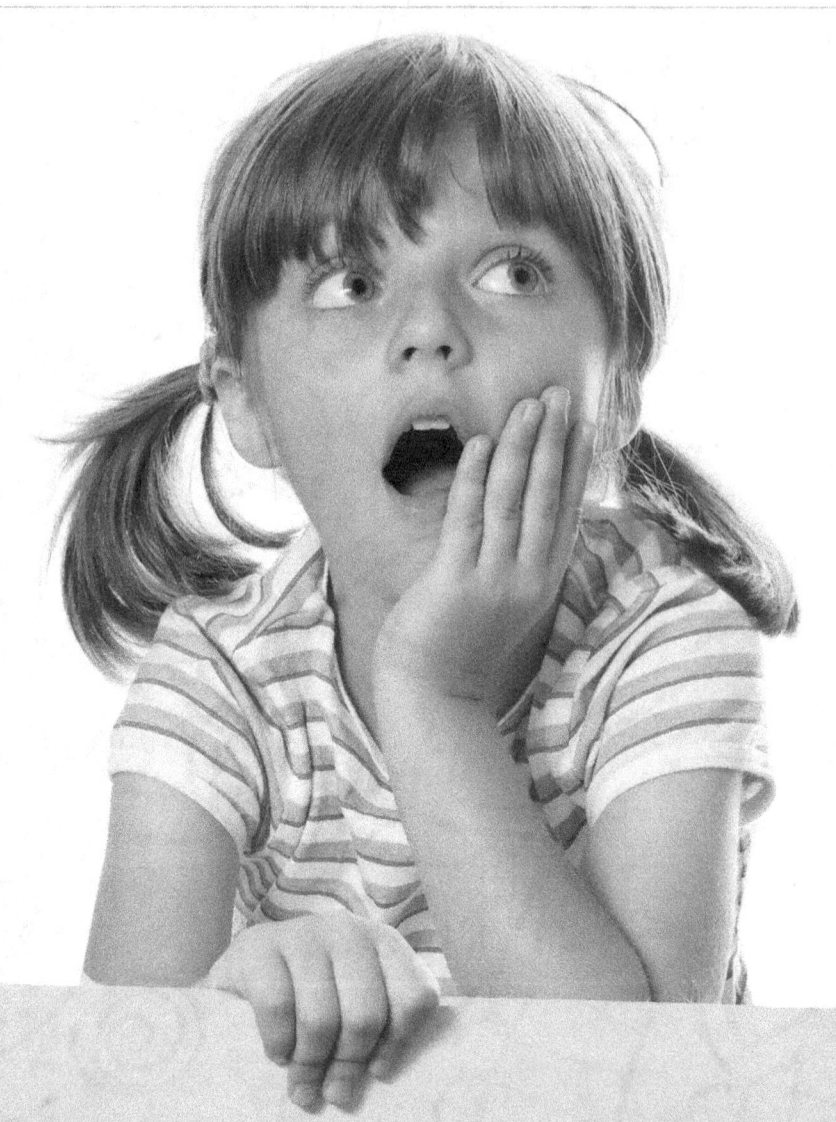

Did you know?
We Have a Great Mailing List!

Free Downloadable Coloring Pages
Monthly Giveaways
Exclusive Discounts
& More!

 SCAN ME

Scan the QR Code or Visit LiltKids.com to Join

thank you

for your purchase!
If you enjoyed this book,
please leave a review. As a
very small independent
book publisher, every
review helps us compete
with larger companies.

scan me

Scan the QR Code
to Leave a Review

(open your phone's camera
and hold it up to the
square)

www.ingramcontent.com/pod-product-compliance
Lightning Source LLC
Chambersburg PA
CBHW081305170526
45165CB00011B/3412